PEOPLE
WHO MADE
A DIFFERENCE

MIKHAIL GORBACHEV

Titles in the
PEOPLE WHO MADE A DIFFERENCE
series include

Louis Braille
Marie Curie
Father Damien
Mahatma Gandhi
Bob Geldof
Mikhail Gorbachev
Martin Luther King, Jr.
Abraham Lincoln
Nelson Mandela
Ralph Nader
Florence Nightingale
Louis Pasteur
Albert Schweitzer
Mother Teresa
Sojourner Truth
Desmond Tutu
Lech Walesa
Raoul Wallenberg

North American edition first published in 1992 by
Gareth Stevens Children's Books
1555 North RiverCenter Drive, Suite 201
Milwaukee, Wisconsin 53212, USA

This edition copyright © 1992 by Gareth Stevens, Inc.;
abridged from *Mikhail Gorbachev: Revolutionary for democracy,*
copyright © 1991 by Exley Publications Ltd. and written by
Anna Sproule. Additional end matter copyright © 1992 by
Gareth Stevens, Inc.

Library of Congress Cataloging-in-Publication Data

Sproule, Anna.
    Mikhail Gorbachev : changing the world order / [abridged by]
Charles R. Bennett, Anna Sproule.
        p. cm. — (People who made a difference)
    Includes index.
    Summary: An account of the life and times of this leader who is
promoting reform in the Soviet Union.
    ISBN 0-8368-0619-0
    1. Gorbachev, Mikhail Sergeyevich, 1931- —Juvenile literature.
2. Heads of state—Soviet Union—Biography—Juvenile literature.
3. Soviet Union—Politics and government—1985- —Juvenile
literature. [1. Gorbachev, Mikhail Sergeyevich, 1931- / 2. Heads
of state.] 3. Soviet Union—Politics and government—1985-]
    I. Bennett, Charles R. (Charles Russell) II. Title. III. Series.
DK290.3.G67S57   1992
947.085'4'092—dc20   C [B]   GoR   91-50542

For a free color catalog describing
Gareth Stevens' list of high-quality
children's books, call

1-800-341-3569 (USA) or
1-800-461-9120 (Canada)

PICTURE CREDITS
Brian Harris 55; The Hulton Photo-
graphic Library 7; Keston College Photo
Archive 33; Magnum Photos Ltd. — Eric
Lessing 6, Ian Berry 18, 25, Henri
Cartier-Bresson 27, Burt Glinn 28, 29,
Franco Zecchin 32, 56 (upper), Peter
Marlow 37, Abbas 58; Novosti 36; Tom
Redman cover illustration; The Society
for Cultural Relations with the USSR 16
(lower), 20, 34, 35, 42, 43, 46; Frank
Spooner Pictures — V. Shone/Gamma 4,
Chip Hires/Gamma 8 (upper), 9 (upper),
Patrick Peal/Gamma 8 (lower), G.
Merrilon/Gamma 9 (lower), Felici/
Gamma 11, A.P.N./Gamma 12, Daniel
Simon/Gamma 13, 30, Novosti/Gamma
22, 40, 41, 48, Blanche/Gamma 41
(upper), Tass/Gamma 41 (lower),
Merrilon/Piel/Gamma 51, Bouvet/
Gamma 53 (upper), Bouvet/Merrilon/
Gamma 53 (lower), Zola/Gamma 56
(lower), Merrilon/Gamma 57 (upper),
Bassinac/Gamma 57 (lower), 60.

Series conceived by Helen Exley
Editor: Amy Bauman
Editorial assistant: Diane Laska

Printed in MEXICO

1 2 3 4 5 6 7 8 9 96 95 94 93 92

**PEOPLE
WHO MADE
A DIFFERENCE**

*Changing the
world order*

MIKHAIL
GORBACHEV

**Russell
Bennett**

**Anna
Sproule**

Gareth Stevens Children's Books
MILWAUKEE

A new era

A wild storm battered the tiny island of Malta. Violent winds whipped through Marsaxlokk Bay, and fifteen-foot waves smashed against the Soviet ship *Maxim Gorky,* anchored at the dock. On board the ship were George Bush, president of the United States, and Mikhail Gorbachev, president of the Soviet Union. It was December 1989.

The leaders of the most powerful countries in the world had come to this island near the southern tip of Italy to talk about peace and trust. After World War II ended in 1945, relations between the two countries had gone bad. A period of mistrust, tension, and fear followed. This period came to be known as the cold war.

After their meeting, the two presidents would tell the world that the cold war was over. They would say that this was the beginning of a new era of relations between the United States and the Soviet Union.

The end of the cold war was just one unbelievable event in a year that was filled with unbelievable changes. During 1989, the Communist governments of Poland,

"Mr. Gorbachev has banished fear."
Rupert Cornwell,
in the Independent,
December 28, 1989

Opposite: George Bush and Mikhail Gorbachev, presidents of the United States and the Soviet Union, meet on the Soviet cruise ship Maxim Gorky *to declare the end of the cold war.*

5

Hungary, East Germany, Czechoslovakia, Bulgaria, and Romania all became democratic. Fear and oppression had been lifted from the heads of 115,000,000 people. These changes could have taken months or even years. But in 1989, they took days or weeks at the most. It was as if the history of Eastern Europe had been put on fast forward.

Prague Spring

In Czechoslovakia, for example, six weeks of protests changed the course of the country. For more than forty years, Czechoslovakia had lived under a government that was controlled by the Soviet Union. The people had no freedoms, and fear was always part of their lives.

But protest against their government was also a part of their lives. In early 1968, protests by the Czech people forced out their cruel government. The new government passed laws that gave the people more freedoms. The laws were known as the "Prague Spring."

The Soviet Union, however, felt that the new laws and freedoms threatened Soviet power. So, in August of 1968, the Soviets sent tanks and troops into Prague, the capital city of Czechoslovakia. The new government was quickly crushed, and the old laws were brought back. The Soviet Union had sent a message to all of the

After World War II, the countries of Eastern Europe fell under the Soviet Union's power. They became part of a huge Communist empire. The man seen above died in Hungary in October 1956 when the people revolted. It took Soviet tanks to crush the revolution.

countries under its control: "Do not question our authority."

Twenty years later, things were different. In fact, the Soviet Union was now on the side of the Czech people.

Prague winter

The magic of 1989 touched Czechoslovakia in November. One Friday after school, tens of thousands of young people marched in the streets of Prague. They wanted freedom and a new government. Police used clubs to stop that march.

But other marches went on. Now 250,000 people were coming into the streets every day. On the eighth day of marches, the

In 1968, the people of Czechoslovakia tried to break free of Soviet Communism. A more liberal government made sweeping changes in a period that was then called Prague Spring. But that August, Soviet troops like these moved in and restored order.

leaders of the Communist party resigned. The protesters sang and danced in the streets, but that was not the end. The new leaders were too much like the old ones, so the marches started again. Ten days later, the prime minister resigned. Three weeks after that, the leader of the protesters became the president of Czechoslovakia. The people were beginning to see their dream of freedom come true.

A prison country

Several weeks before the events in

At the Berlin Wall.
Opposite, top: With
hammer and chisel, a
young Berliner chips
away at the wall.
Opposite, below:
Crosses at the foot of the
wall honor some of the
people who tried to
escape over it.
Above and left: A
weeping woman and a
smiling soldier show
two faces of joy as the
wall opens.

Czechoslovakia took place, change also came to East Germany. After World War II, Germany was divided in two. A democratic government was set up in West Germany. In East Germany, a Communist government ruled. Even Berlin, the capital of Germany, was divided in half.

There were almost no freedoms in East Germany. Few people were allowed to leave the country. Anyone who said anything against the government could be put in jail. In Berlin, however, it was possible to get to freedom on the west side of the city. So, in 1961, the Communists built a wall down the middle of the city. The ugly concrete wall was lined with watchtowers and armed guards. The German people had always been proud of their capital. The Berlin Wall was an insult and a disgrace. It stood for everything that was bad about the East German government.

The wall tumbles down

The summer of 1989 was coming to an end. People all over Europe were returning from their vacations. East Germans had been allowed to travel to Hungary, a Communist country. Hungary had agreed to make sure that all vacationers returned to East Germany. But in this year of change, Hungary had new freedoms. Among these was the freedom to leave the country. Suddenly, the East Germans vacationing in Hungary saw their chance. Many of them traveled beyond Hungary to freedom in Austria.

In East Germany, the people held demonstrations against the government all through October. On November 4, half a million people gathered in East Berlin to demand changes. A few days later, all the top East German officials resigned. The leader of the country promised to change the entire government.

Then, on November 9, the impossible happened. To calm the people, East

Germany opened the hated Berlin Wall. As bulldozers broke into the concrete, people streamed through. Others climbed over the top. Church bells rang and car horns blasted. People all over Germany laughed, cheered, and cried. They were ready to start a new life.

The pope and the president

The changes that swept Eastern Europe in 1989 were made possible mainly through the work of one man: Mikhail Gorbachev, president of the Soviet Union.

Gorbachev had become the leader of the Soviet Union in 1985. Since then, the changes that he had put in place in his

Pope John Paul II meets Mikhail and Raisa Gorbachev.

Above: Rows of tanks rumble through Moscow's Red Square on the anniversary of the Russian Revolution of 1917. Opposite: A huge portrait of V. I. Lenin surveys the scene.

own country had set an example for all of Eastern Europe. So it was fitting that the end of the cold war also came about in a year of so many changes.

On his way to Malta to see President Bush, Gorbachev stopped in Rome, Italy. There, he and his wife, Raisa, visited Pope John Paul II, the head of the Catholic church. It would be the first time that a pope and the head of the Soviet Union had met in over seventy years. During that time, the Soviet people had been persecuted for practicing religion.

Gorbachev promised the pope that there would be religious freedom for all people in the Soviet Union. He also invited the pope to visit Moscow. The meeting lasted for more than an hour. Then Gorbachev boarded an airplane for Malta.

New freedoms and new directions

Mikhail Gorbachev was the spirit behind the revolutionary changes in the Communist world in 1989. He was the author of changes that had been going on in the Soviet Union for five years.

When he became the Soviet leader in 1985, Gorbachev wanted to give freedoms to his people. He also wanted to rebuild the Soviet government and economic system. He used two words to describe his plans for the nation — glasnost and perestroika. *Glasnost* is the Russian word that means "openness." *Perestroika* means "rebuilding." Gorbachev's plans would soon touch people in the rest of the world.

For years, people in the West feared the Soviet Union. They were afraid that the cold war would become "hot." That could mean a nuclear war that could destroy the world. But in a short time, people saw that Gorbachev wanted peace in the world as much as he wanted change within the Soviet Union. He himself said that "There would be neither winners nor losers in such a war. There would be no survivors."

Mikhail "Misha" Gorbachev stands between his maternal grandparents in a Privolnoye backyard.

The man with the iron teeth

At the end of the 1980s, Mikhail Gorbachev was one of the two most powerful people in the world. But even then, he did not seem like a man who would change history. He was a pleasant man with a warm smile and a friendly manner. Yet he was also a man of courage, strength, and intelligence. One of his gifts was the toughness with which he pursued his goals. It was once said that he "has a nice smile, but he has teeth of iron." After five years as president, Gorbachev had accomplished many of his goals for the country. But many people felt that he was moving too slowly.

Misha

Mikhail Sergeyevich Gorbachev was born in the village of Privolnoye. This village is found in the southwest corner of the Soviet Union in the Stavropol region. This region produces most of the country's food. For part of the year, the hills surrounding the village are covered by fields of grain. Even now, Privolnoye is a simple village that has only one paved street.

Gorbachev, called Misha by his family, was born on March 2, 1931, in his parents' two-room house. His parents were peasant farmers. His father also repaired and operated farm machines.

Misha was born in hard times. People were poor, and there was never enough food. But the cruel government, headed by Joseph Stalin, was another problem. Stalin had been the country's leader since shortly after the Russian Revolution.

Joseph Stalin was born Iosif Dzhugashvili. He took the name Stalin, meaning "man of steel," when he entered politics.

Revolution

For hundreds of years, the Soviet Union had been ruled by leaders known as czars. In this country, which was then called Russia, life was hard for the common people. This led to revolution in 1917, and communists took over the government. The new leader was Vladimir Ilyich Lenin. Joseph Stalin was one of his assistants.

Above: This painting shows the death of a policeman as the Russian Revolution of 1917 burst to life. The rulers of Russia had repressed the people for centuries.

Right: In this poster from 1920, a man and a woman working over an anvil illustrate the communist ideals of courage, work, and fellowship.

One of the first things Lenin did was take over all property. That meant that the government owned all farms, factories, and railroads. This new system was hardly in place when civil war broke out in 1918. In this war, the communists fought against people who still supported the czar. This bitter war lasted until 1921, when the rebels were defeated.

By this time, the country was in ruin. The government-run economy was not producing enough food or goods. Everywhere, people were restless and angry. Lenin was forced to return many factories and farms to private owners.

Stalin's plans

When Lenin died in 1924, Stalin became the leader. Stalin felt it was important for the Soviet Union's industry to catch up with the rest of the world's. Factories began producing iron and steel and electrical power. They manufactured trains, farm equipment, and other large machines. But the factories did not make goods that people could buy for themselves. This meant there were no cars, refrigerators, or radios. Even houses and clothing were in short supply.

The new industrial growth created a food problem. To work in the factories, many people had moved to the cities. As the city populations grew, they needed more food. To solve the problem, the

World War II comes to the Soviet Union. In this 1941 photo, victims of Nazi terror lie scattered across an open field. Soviet women search among the dead for bodies of family members and friends. During the war, twenty million Soviets died.

government again took control of the farms. Small farms were combined into large farms called collectives. Peasants were forced to work on the collectives just as if they had a job at a factory.

Resistance, hunger, and death

The peasants did not like their new life. Some refused to work on the collectives. Some killed their farm animals rather than sell them to the government. Stalin reacted with an iron fist. Anyone who did not cooperate with his plan was executed or sent to a prison camp.

As the industrial boom continued, so did the need for food. The government took more and more of what the collective farms grew. In 1931, the year Misha was born, the government took about two-thirds of the farmers' grain. A bad harvest that year pushed the country into a famine. The following winter was a disaster. In some villages, all the children under two years of age died of hunger. In Misha's region alone, about fifty thousand people died. It is estimated that between 1931 and 1933, more than fourteen million people died of starvation or were executed by the government.

In the 1940s, Soviet farm workers bring in the harvest.

War and school

In the fall of 1939, Misha started primary school. World War II began at the same time, and Germany invaded the Soviet Union two years later. The fighting, however, did not reach the Stavropol region before the war ended in 1945.

That same year, Misha began his farm work. Because so many people had died in the war, the government ordered all children over the age of twelve to spend fifty days a year working on a collective. There, the children helped care for and harvest the crops. Misha worked long, hard days on the farm.

The first time Misha was away from Privolnoye was when he went to high school. Each day he walked ten miles (16 km) to school. There, Misha got excellent grades, and his teachers remember that he was interested in many things. In school, he led the Young Communist League, or Komsomol, and was a member of the drama club. His high school girlfriend, Yulia Karagodina, recalls that he was a good actor and dominated the stage. In one show, he even played a czar. Out of school, he continued his work on the farm. The year before he graduated, Privolnoye had a good harvest. For his work on the collective, Misha won the Order of Red Banner of Labor. It was unusual for an eighteen-year-old to win the honor.

Misha's forcefulness and confidence were already showing in high school. Yulia remembers that he sometimes argued with

Mikhail Gorbachev attended Moscow State University (seen below) in the 1950s. Gorbachev had his first contact with big-city life and foreigners at the school. He also met his wife, Raisa, there.

teachers if he felt he was right. Once, he challenged a history teacher who he thought was a very poor instructor. Misha shouted: "Do you want to keep your teaching certificate?" Protected by his self-confidence, he survived this battle and went on to fight others.

Years later, Yulia would recall that "He was the sort of man who felt he was right and could prove it to anyone."

A new world

Mikhail Gorbachev's life changed dramatically in 1950. He had graduated from high school and enrolled in Moscow State University. Now the man from the country village who had lived in a small house made of clay and wood was moving to the largest city in the country. Moscow was the center of Soviet culture and political power. It was the heart of the Soviet Union.

Moscow is about one thousand miles (1,600 km) from Privolnoye. Along the way, Mikhail saw the destruction that World War II had caused. The war had been over for five years, but much of the country was still in ruins.

At the university, Mikhail enrolled in the law school. That seemed an odd choice. At the time, very few students studied law. Years later, one of his classmates said that Mikhail was more interested in public affairs than in law.

"Working people were justly indignant at the behavior of people who, enjoying trust and responsibility, abused power, suppressed criticism, made fortunes and, in some cases, even became accomplices in . . . criminal acts."
Mikhail Gorbachev, describing the Soviet Union under Leonid Brezhnev in Gorbachev's book Perestroika

21

At the university, Mikhail met people from all over the Soviet Union and Europe. It was the first time he had gotten to know people from outside his small farming community. Like many students interested in politics, Mikhail was active in the Komsomol. Before long, he became the *komsorg*, or Komsomol leader, of his class. Within two years, he was the *komsorg* of the whole law school.

Gorbachev's roommate was from Czechoslovakia. His name was Zdenek Mlynar. Years later, Mlynar would be one of the Czechs behind the Prague Spring. Mlynar taught Gorbachev much about Western life-style. The two were close friends and talked endlessly.

Once, they had seen a movie that painted a glowing picture of life on a collective. Gorbachev later told Mlynar that he thought the movie was wrong. At that time, it was unusual and risky for anyone to say anything against the government. As leader of the government, Joseph Stalin carried out his policies through threats, terror, and force. What he said was the law, was the official law. What he said was history, was the official history. Anyone who dared to disagree with him could be killed or sent to the Gulag. The Gulag was a series of prison camps.

Gorbachev showed great trust in his friend to have made such a comment. He also showed the beginnings of what later

Mikhail Gorbachev was an energetic, intelligent, self-confident student who spoke well in public. Even as a young man, he had many of the marks of a politician.

would be his passion to correct and change the Soviet system.

At the university, Gorbachev met and fell in love with his future wife. One evening, Mikhail had gone to a dancing school to poke fun at some of his friends who were taking lessons there. At the school, he met a beautiful, intelligent woman named Raisa Titorenko. Raisa was a philosophy student who enjoyed reading all kinds of books. The two were married in Mikhail's last year at Moscow State University.

Going home

In the fall of 1955, Mikhail and Raisa Gorbachev moved to his homeland in southern Russia. They settled in the city of Stavropol, the capital of the Stavropol region. There, Raisa began work as a teacher. Mikhail, however, did not immediately go to work as a lawyer. It is doubtful that he ever wanted to work as a lawyer, although this is what he had studied to do.

Gorbachev's interest in politics led him to go to work for the Communist party. He soon landed a job in the propaganda department of the local Komsomol. In this job, he visited local branches of the youth movement, organized meetings, and spoke at youth conferences.

Gorbachev was popular and respected in his region. Promotions came quickly

"I was 20. . . . They [the KGB] came to me and said they'd appreciate it if I'd tell them what the foreign students did, what their interests were and what vices they had. . . . In the end, after getting practically zero information out of me, the KGB fired me."
Vladimir Ashkenazy,
conductor and pianist,
in the Times (London),
February 10, 1990

for him. Within a year, he was named secretary of the Komsomol. Two years later, in 1958, he was promoted to first secretary. That was the top job in the Stavropol Komsomol.

Moving up

Gorbachev's job also put him in touch with officials in other, nearby regions. Many of these people would later be helpful as his career moved ahead. Gorbachev was energetic and ambitious. But he was also thirty years old. He had been working in the communist youth organization since high school. It was time for a change.

In 1962, Gorbachev took a new job as an agricultural official for the Communist party. It was now his job to manage everything that was produced by all the farms in his region. Gorbachev knew that his farm experience would not be enough for this new job. So he began a correspondence course at the Stavropol Institute of Agriculture. Five years later, he received a degree in agricultural economics. That same year, Raisa received a doctorate degree.

Gorbachev had been moving up through the ranks of the local party all along. Now, with his new degree, he moved even faster. In 1970, thirty-nine-year old Gorbachev was promoted to the top job in the Stavropol Communist party.

He was First Party Secretary. He had reached the top of the ladder in Stavropol.

Draped in plastic to keep the rain off, Soviet shoppers examine vegetables in a market.

Back to the center

Gorbachev soon found new ladders. As the head of the Communist party in Stavropol, he had to work with party leaders in Moscow. In 1971, he became even closer to those leaders. He became a member of the party's Central Committee. The Central Committee was in charge of the activities of the party. Three years later, Gorbachev also became Stavropol's representative in the Soviet legislature. This body is called the Supreme Soviet.

Then, in 1978, Gorbachev got the biggest boost of his career. The party needed a new Central Committee secretary for agriculture. This was the person who would run the agriculture programs of the whole country. The party leaders were having a difficult time making a choice. None of the candidates seemed quite right.

Then Gorbachev's name came up. The leaders knew Gorbachev because they had met him when they visited his region. Everyone agreed that he worked hard and did his job well. Also, he wasn't anyone's enemy. He didn't seem as if he would cause trouble for the party. In short, he seemed like the right person for the job.

The leaders made their decision. The job went to Gorbachev. In December, Mikhail and Raisa Gorbachev moved back to Moscow. At age forty-seven, Mikhail Gorbachev had returned to the center of Soviet power.

The party and the government

Until recently, the Soviet Union had been run by two separate organizations. One was the Communist party, which had some fifteen million members. The party had been the strongest force in the country for a long time. Its job was to decide on the laws and policies of the nation. The other organization was the government. It was

"The greatest difficulty in our restructuring effort lies in our thinking."
Mikhail Gorbachev,
in Perestroika

the government's job to carry out the laws and policies set by the party.

The party and the government each had its own leader. The head of the government was the president. The head of the party was the general secretary, who led the party's powerful Central Committee. Now Gorbachev was part of that committee.

How the economy works

In the Soviet Union, the state, which had always been run by these two organizations, owned all the land. The

A hard and rugged life: Soviet women wash clothes through a hole in the ice.

state also owned the railroads, factories, machines, power plants, natural resources, and everything else used to produce goods and services for the people.

The state planned what and how much to produce. For example, it decided how much meat, grain, gasoline, clothing, and electricity to produce. The state set all prices and employed all workers. The system was supposed to do the most good for the most people. But as Gorbachev saw in the 1970s, it was not working for the ordinary Soviet people.

The long wait

For most people, life was a struggle. Most basic goods were often in short supply.

Often the shortages were caused by a mistake in the government's plan. Other times, a factory did not get the parts or materials it needed. Also, it was not unusual for goods to leave a factory but never get to the stores. Goods were often lost or stolen.

When the goods did come into the government stores, people had to wait in line to buy them. They waited for almost everything: food, soap, toys, winter boots. For a very scarce item, such as carpets, shoppers might have to stand in line all day. To make matters worse, many goods were not well made. Refrigerators didn't freeze things. Heaters didn't heat. Boots fell apart in the snow. The quality of goods was often bad because factories were under pressure to meet quotas. Factory managers often did not watch the quality if that meant not making a quota.

One way to get certain items was through the "black market." The black market was an illegal way of selling goods. Prices were very high, though. Most people could not afford them.

In one area, however, the Soviet Union became an industrial giant. The nation built many dams and canals and began producing great amounts of iron and steel, oil, natural gas, electricity, railroads, ships, and trucks. These things, however, had little effect on the everyday lives of ordinary people. Life for them was bleak.

Leonid Brezhnev (left), former leader of the Soviet Union, talks with other party leaders while at a parade in Moscow's Red Square.

The new privileged few

The Soviet system was supposed to provide for all people. It was also supposed to be classless. That meant that no one group of people would have any more wealth or privileges that any other group.

But after Stalin came to power, a new class came into being. The class was made up of the political leaders of the country. By the time Leonid Brezhnev became general secretary in 1964, this new upper class had many privileges that average people didn't.

The people had little hope that their lives would get better or that the Soviet system would change. They felt powerless to do anything about their situation.

Crimes and punishments

After Stalin died, Soviet society became freer. But when Brezhnev came to power, it tightened again. By the late 1970s, most of Stalin's terror policies had been dropped. But it was still a crime to question or criticize the party, and police or spies for the party were ready to arrest anyone who did.

The prisons and work camps of the Gulag still waited for people who committed such crimes. It is estimated that at this time, the work camps still held about two million people.

But the Gulag was not the worst punishment a person could get. Some

"There is virtually no unemployment. . . . Health care is free, and so is education. . . . and we are proud of this. But we also see that dishonest people try to exploit these advantages . . . they know only their rights, but they do not want to know their duties. . . ."
Mikhail Gorbachev,
on the Brezhnev legacy,
in Perestroika

political prisoners were sent to mental hospitals where doctors were forced to declare them insane. In these hospitals, the patients were treated badly and had no hope of being freed.

Citizens who criticized the party but were well known to the public presented a special problem. The government had to use other ways to silence these people, and they found them. For example, Aleksandr Solzhenitsyn wrote novels that the government did not like. One of his books, *Gulag Archipelago*, is a story of the terrible conditions in the work camps. The government took Solzhenitsyn's

A modern Soviet mental hospital is seen below. The government kept some political prisoners in hospitals such as this, claiming they needed "medical treatment."

citizenship away and forced him to leave the country.

Even people who supported such rebels were punished. Mstislav Rostropovich is a world famous cello player. His wife, Galina, was a star of the Bolshoi Opera. Both of these people defended Solzhenitsyn. Before long, Mstislav's concerts were canceled, and his work was no longer heard on the radio. The same thing happened to Galina. In the end, their citizenship was taken away, and they left the Soviet Union.

As the 1970s turned into the 1980s, shortages, police spies, and the work

A photograph from 1971 captures the despair of "psychiatric patient" Yuri Titov. Titov was a member of the Soviet secret police who became a Christian. He was imprisoned for his beliefs.

camps were terrible aspects of Soviet life. Across the Soviet Union, people were dissatisfied and unhappy. This was the troubled nation that Mikhail Gorbachev, as a secretary of the Central Committee, was to help rule.

The harvests that failed

Of all the high positions in the party, secretary for agriculture had a record of failure. The Soviet Union was a huge country and much could go wrong. And it usually did.

Right away, it went wrong for Gorbachev. The winter of 1978 was hard, and the next summer was hot. The harvest of 1979 was bad. The Soviet Union had to buy grain from other countries to feed the people. The next year's harvest was also bad, and the 1981 harvest was horrible. Gorbachev had tried to improve the farm system, but he couldn't fight poor harvests. The 1982 harvest was only slightly better. Gorbachev would have to deliver the bad news to the party. He would almost certainly be blamed for the shortages.

Then something happened that saved Gorbachev's job. Leonid Brezhnev died. As the party scrambled about trying to find a new leader, the bad farm situation was forgotten.

The new general secretary was Yuri Andropov. Andropov had plans for big changes in the Soviet system. First, he was going to shake up the Communist party. He wanted to reduce the leaders' special privileges. He also wanted to get rid of officials who did not do their jobs.

Andropov's plans were cut short when he became sick a few months later. As he got worse, he realized that he needed someone who could take his place when he could not go to meetings or make speeches. He chose Mikhail Gorbachev.

Boris Pasternak (above) was the author of the world-famous novel Doctor Zhivago. *Pasternak was not popular with the Soviet government, and he had to smuggle his book to Italy to get it published. When he died in 1960, Soviets crowded to his funeral (opposite).*

The travels of "Mr. G"

Gorbachev was now one of the most

Above: When Mikhail Gorbachev came to power, his official portraits showed him without the birthmark on his forehead.

Opposite: "Mr. G" greets well-wishers in London. His habit of shaking hands with people in crowds pleased Westerners.

important men in the country. He was also becoming known in the West. In 1983, he traveled to Canada. The reporters were used to serious, reserved, quiet Soviet officials. They were surprised to find that Gorbachev was outgoing. He enjoyed meeting people, and he liked discussions.

The next year, Gorbachev visited England. The British found him not just open; he was friendly. The British press began calling him "Mr. G.," and Prime Minister Margaret Thatcher said that Gorbachev was someone she "could do business with." The Soviet Union was supposed to be the feared enemy of the West and its way of life. Gorbachev was changing that image wherever he went.

End of an era

In early 1984, Andropov died. The new general secretary of the Communist party was Konstantin Chernenko. He was seventy-two years old and sick when he took the job. He could barely make a speech at Andropov's funeral. A year later, it was Chernenko who was being buried. Behind his coffin stood the new general secretary of the Communist party: Mikhail Sergeyevich Gorbachev.

The country that Gorbachev took over in 1985 stretched from the Baltic Sea to the Pacific Ocean. It had fifteen republics and about 300 million people. It was about the same size as the United States, Canada,

and Central America combined. Its power, however, extended much farther than its physical borders and included control over the Eastern bloc countries. This name referred to the countries along the Soviet Union's western border: East Germany, Poland, Czechoslovakia, Hungary, Romania, Bulgaria, and Albania. These countries and the Soviet Union shared the same economic and social problems.

Beyond the Eastern bloc was the West. For years, the Western countries had feared and mistrusted the Soviet Union. And the Soviet Union had feared and mistrusted them. The two sides had been locked in a weapons race. That was the situation Gorbachev stepped into when he became general secretary in 1985.

Gorbachev poses with his daughter, Irina.

Beginning at home

The Soviet Union was a troubled nation. The first thing Gorbachev did was change some of the leaders. He replaced many of the old guard with people he trusted and respected. But even this did not guarantee that the government would run smoothly, Gorbachev found out. Some of these same people would later try to overthrow him.

One of the next things he did was crack down on drinking. Alcoholism was a serious, growing problem in the country. It affected factory and farm production and could be linked to many crimes. Gorbachev felt that attacking alcoholism was a modest but dramatic way to begin his task.

Perestroika

It was clear to Gorbachev that the Soviet Union had lost its way. The trouble seemed to come from the way the Soviet economy worked. New economic plans that were managed better might solve this problem.

But Gorbachev had another idea. This plan called for the party to loosen the system. If the party would allow private business, it would create competition. Competition would drive people to work harder and produce more goods of better quality. Gorbachev used the word *perestroika* to sum up this method. It means "restructuring" or "rebuilding."

Gorbachev told the people that to make this plan work, they would have to work "an extra bit harder." In a book he wrote on his plan, he said, "I like this phrase . . . it is not just a slogan, but a . . . state of mind. Any job one takes on must be grasped and felt with one's soul, mind, and heart."

He explained that perestroika meant expecting more of everyone in the nation. It meant making industry and agriculture more efficient. And it meant paying attention to what ordinary people wanted.

Glasnost

Gorbachev's plan also meant having courage — the courage to change, to face

One of Gorbachev's strengths is his ability to talk with people. He is equally at ease when walking in crowds (above), talking with workers at a Chernobyl nuclear power plant (opposite, top), or drinking tea in someone's living room (opposite, bottom).

criticism, and to be honest and open. For almost seventy years, the government had not been honest with the people. And the people had not been allowed to express their feelings about the government. That had to stop.

Gorbachev used the word *glasnost* to describe what he meant. It means "openness." He pointed out that the Soviet Union needed openness about public affairs in every sphere of life. He felt that everyone should know what is good as

well as what is bad in order to build the good and fight the bad. Before long, people all over the world knew the Russian words glasnost and perestroika.

Openness and restructuring were Gorbachev's solutions for his sick country. But even Gorbachev found these revolutionary ideas hard to put into practice. His first chance came on April 26, 1986. That day, a nuclear power plant in the small city of Chernobyl exploded. A huge radioactive cloud spread over the

"An individual must know and feel that his contribution is needed, that his dignity is not being infringed upon, that he is being treated with trust and respect."
Mikhail Gorbachev,
in Perestroika

area. This accident is now considered the world's worst nuclear disaster.

At first, Gorbachev did not live up to his own standards. The state did not tell the world anything about the accident until three days later. Then something had to be said because scientists in Sweden had detected the radioactive dust in the air.

It was more than two weeks before Gorbachev himself spoke to the world about the explosion. Many people were disappointed. They felt that Gorbachev should not have gone back to the old Soviet ways of hiding things. Glasnost was off to a rocky start.

In April 1986, a nuclear reactor at Chernobyl exploded (opposite). Radioactive material spread west as far as England. Over 100 thousand people in the area had to leave their homes (below).

Shifting gears

But openness was a new experience for the Soviet people and their leaders. As they got used to the idea, it did work. The coming months brought proof.

In August 1986, a newspaper in the republic of Estonia printed a story about the Soviet soldiers in Chernobyl. It said the men were afraid of the radiation and that they had gone on strike. A story like that would not have been allowed to be printed a few years earlier.

Andrei Sakharov is another example. Sakharov was a nuclear physicist whose work had won a Nobel Prize. Despite his work, Sakharov had been confined to the city of Gorky as punishment for speaking out against the government. There, police watched and harassed him. In December 1986, he was freed.

In January 1987, a top officer was fired from the secret police, called the Komitet Gosudarstvennoy Bezopasnosti (KGB). The officer had made false charges against a reporter who had spoken against communism. In the old days, that had been the KGB way of doing things. A month later, the government freed 150 political prisoners, and many more would soon follow.

In 1988, glasnost touched Soviet school children. Their final test in history had been canceled. The reason was that the textbooks they had been using were being

rewritten. The new books would tell the truth about Soviet history.

Not so evil

And so the pressure in the Soviet Union eased. At the same time, the cold war with the West was beginning to thaw.

Raising the Soviet standard of living was one of Gorbachev's main goals. That would take money, though. For years, much of the Soviet government's money had been spent on weapons. If fewer arms were needed, money could be used for the people. For the Soviet Union to cut back on arms, however, the United States would also have to cut back. This meant that these two countries would have to trust each other.

U.S. president Ronald Reagan had thought of the Soviet Union as the "evil

In this 1960 photo, rows of nuclear missiles are wheeled into Red Square on the first day of May, or May Day, a holiday in the Soviet Union.

empire." Gorbachev changed that. The two leaders had two meetings between 1985 and 1986. No real agreements were made, but the men found that they liked each other.

In December 1987, Gorbachev came to Washington, D.C. This time something was accomplished. The two leaders signed a treaty. It was an agreement to cut back the size of both countries' huge stores of nuclear missiles. Talking about the treaty, Gorbachev said, "We can be proud of planting this sapling, which may one day grow into a mighty tree of peace."

Reagan, perhaps still a little doubtful, repeated something that he had said before: "Trust — but check."

Gorbachev joked, "You repeat that at every meeting." The people who were in the room laughed and applauded.

"Gradually, as though thawing, our newspapers, magazines, radio and television are uncovering and handling new topics."
Mikhail Gorbachev,
in Perestroika

The plan stalls

Perestroika was moving ahead slowly. In June of 1987, the Supreme Soviet had passed Gorbachev's economic program. But Soviets still disagreed about many of Gorbachev's changes. Some felt that his plan was too mild. This included a man named Boris Yeltsin. Yeltsin had once supported Gorbachev but was now one of his harshest critics. Yeltsin wanted the changes to be stronger and come faster.

Others, however, did not like the plan or perestroika at all. People such as the party

Mikhail Gorbachev and Ronald Reagan sign a treaty to reduce the numbers of nuclear missiles that each country holds.

leaders were not content. They were set in their ways and did not want change. Some of these people felt that Gorbachev was destroying Soviet achievements as he tried to destroy the evils.

As powerful as Gorbachev was, he was not safe from enemies in the party. To protect himself and his plan, he began to fire the critics from their high-level jobs.

Free elections!

Gorbachev dealt with the people in another way. In the summer of 1988, he called a special meeting of party members. Five thousand members from all over the nation came to Moscow. Meetings between the general secretary and ordinary party members were rare. This was the first in more than forty-five years.

At the Palace of Congresses, Gorbachev announced a new part of his plan: "We are learning democracy and glasnost, learning to argue and conduct a debate, to tell one another the truth." Democracy meant that the people took part in the government. Democracy meant that the people should have a voice in the Supreme Soviet. Democracy meant free elections.

Free elections were something new for the Soviet people. In the past, people had been forced to vote. But for each position, the party had chosen only one candidate. It had all been for show. It was the old Soviet way.

"The nations of the world resemble today a pack of mountaineers tied together by a climbing rope. They can either climb on together to the mountain peak or fall together into an abyss."
Mikhail Gorbachev,
in Perestroika

The five thousand party members took these amazing proposals calmly. There was applause in just the right places, but that was all.

Nothing was calm on March 26, 1989, though. That was the day of the first free election. In most areas, voters chose between two candidates. In some, there were three. In some cases, the results surprised everyone. In Leningrad, the people voted out the city party leader and his assistant. They also rejected the mayor and his assistant. At long last, the old structure was beginning to crumble.

Let the fresh air in

The year 1989 was a year for the world to remember. In this year, the forty-seven-year-old cold war between the world's two most powerful countries had ended. The Soviet Union was moving — slowly — toward a democratic government and a capitalistic economy. It was also the year that six countries in Eastern Europe threw out their Communist governments and turned to democracy.

In a big way, Mikhail Gorbachev was behind all the changes of 1989. He had opened the door for them in April 1987. At that time, Gorbachev was in Prague, Czechoslovakia, to give a speech on what he thought the relations between Communist countries should be. He suggested that the other countries should

"Perestroika itself can only come through democracy."
Mikhail Gorbachev,
in Perestroika

Opposite: A woman casts her vote in the first real free election ever held in the Soviet Union.

49

follow the lead of the Soviet Union. They should consider glasnost and perestroika for themselves. Gorbachev wanted to direct and persuade the countries. But he didn't want to push them.

Czech leaders were not happy with the speech. But the people applauded it and were warm to Gorbachev. The East German government was cool to the speech. In Bulgaria, the leaders said they already had their own kind of perestroika and glasnost. The president of Romania attacked the speech, and it was censored in the newspapers. Only the governments of Hungary and Poland praised the speech. Their situations, however, were different from the others'. Democratic reforms had had a head start there.

Poland

Poland's new day had actually begun almost ten years before. In 1980, workers in a shipyard there had gone on strike. The strikes spread to other areas, and the country came to a standstill. To end the strike, the government met many of the workers' demands. One was the creation of an independent union. It was called Solidarity. Its leader was Lech Walesa.

Over the coming years, Solidarity led opposition to the government. By 1988, Solidarity had won. Free elections were held, and Solidarity candidates won more than half the seats in Poland's legislature.

Finally, in 1991, Lech Walesa was elected president of Poland.

Hungary

Economic reforms had actually begun in Hungary years before. Protests calling for democracy, however, did not come until 1987. After two years of small changes came a big change, in October 1989. Hungary's parliament officially dissolved the Communist party and declared the country to be a free republic.

Germany

The Berlin Wall tells the whole story. After

Former East German leader Erich Honecker talks with Gorbachev during East Germany's birthday celebration. Barely a month later, the Berlin Wall was down, and Honecker had resigned.

years of being almost prisoners in their own country, East Germans began to protest in the fall of 1989. By the end of October, hundreds of thousands of people took to the streets every day. They demanded freedom. On November 9, the Berlin Wall was torn down. The symbol of East Germany's oppression was taken away. Within a year, Germany was again one country.

Bulgaria

Change in Bulgaria was not so dramatic as it was in some of the other Eastern European countries. It made its move to freedom the day after the Berlin Wall came down. Todor Zhivkov, the country's dictator for thirty-five years, resigned.

Czechoslovakia

The Czechs, too, gained their freedom in November 1989. Twenty-one years before, in 1968, Prague had been the scene of bloodshed. Early that year, liberal leaders made some democratic reforms in the government. The Soviet Union, however, did not want the changes. In August, it sent tanks and troops into the capital city. The new government was crushed.

In 1989, though, demonstrations in the streets of Prague forced the old government out once again. Three days before the end of the year, protest leader Vaclav Havel was elected president.

Romania

Freedom in Romania came with guns and blood. The president, Nicolae Ceausescu, had ruled brutally for over twenty years. Protests against the government in winter 1989 were met by force from the army. The protests spread, and armed fighting broke out in many cities. On December 23, the president was captured. Two days later, after a trial, he and his wife were executed.

What next?

By the first days of the 1990s, Gorbachev had taken the Soviet Union a long way. In February that year, he asked the Central Committee to give up some of the party's

power and allow other political parties to exist. After debating for two days, the committee agreed. This was an amazing step for the party to take. Since 1917, it had in a sense been the government, church, social, and cultural leader of 300 million Soviet people. Now that hold was beginning to break. As usual, the conservative old guard did not want any change. And, as usual, the liberals said Gorbachev had not gone far enough fast enough.

Three days that shook the world

For six years, Gorbachev had shaped and led events in Eastern Europe and in the Soviet Union. But in the summer of 1991, events seemed to outrun Gorbachev. On August 18, a group of traditional Soviet leaders tried to take control of the government. Leaders of the takeover, or coup, surprised Gorbachev at his vacation house in the Crimea and demanded that he surrender his powers. Gorbachev refused.

On Monday, August 19, soldiers and tanks rolled into Moscow. The coup leaders took over the country's radio and television stations. They announced that Gorbachev was ill and that his vice president was in charge of the country. Boris Yeltsin, the president of the Russian republic, spoke out against the coup and urged the Soviet people to resist. Yeltsin was in the parliament building, and people built barricades outside to protect him.

Opposite: Prague, Czechoslovakia. Huge crowds of people pack Wenceslas Square during Czechoslovakia's revolution of 1989.

54

The longing for freedom also affected the Soviet republics of Lithuania, Latvia, and Estonia. Above, in protest against Soviet control, people form a human chain stretching 350 miles (560 km) through the three republics.

Right: Another republic, another protest. In the deeply religious Ukraine, Catholics proclaim their faith. In 1989, Gorbachev gave the people the freedom to worship.

By Tuesday, the coup was already losing strength. About 150,000 people in Moscow and 200,000 in Leningrad demonstrated against the coup. Leaders of other republics also rejected the coup. On

Two kinds of weapons. In Bucharest, Romania (above), people used guns to gain freedom. Meanwhile, in Prague, Czechoslovakia (left), people used roses. Nonviolence helped the Czech people in their revolution because it won public support.

57

In the republic of Turkmenistan, an old man prays in a local mosque. By 1990, the Muslims in the southern republics were beginning to seek independence from the Soviet Union.

Wednesday, the tanks and troops were leaving Moscow, and the coup leaders were trying to escape. By that evening, Gorbachev was back in Moscow.

The coup had seemed doomed from the start, but it shook Gorbachev into action. Within a few days, he had resigned from the Communist party and had disbanded the Central Committee. The party would have no part in the future of the Soviet Union. He also announced that reforms would move much faster.

But the coup had weakened Gorbachev's power and increased Yeltsin's. The two leaders now formed a partnership to rule the country. But it was not clear what the country was to be or how it would finally be governed. Republics were declaring independence from the Union. In fact, by the end of September 1991, Latvia, Lithuania, and Estonia had been accepted as independent countries by the governments of the world.

By the end of 1991, the remaining Soviet republics pushed even harder for total independence. On December 25, Gorbachev stepped down as president, and the Soviet Union was no longer a union. Most of the fifteen former Soviet republics would form a group of nations known as the Commonwealth of Independent States. With Russia as its largest member, these nations would continue to share economic and political interests. But the hammer and sickle of Soviet communism would fly no more.

Mikhail Gorbachev was now out of the political picture, but not before he had given the Soviet people four great gifts. Three of these were the freedom to break away, the freedom to speak one's mind, and the freedom to make changes. In a way, the fourth gift was even greater than freedom. For the first time in the nation's history, a ruler had respected the people's right to respect themselves — to be themselves, to make their own decisions, and to live their lives in dignity and peace.

To find out more . . .

Organizations

The groups listed below can give you more information about the Soviet Union, communism, and Mikhail Gorbachev. When you write to them, tell them exactly what you would like to know, and include your name, address, and age.

Friends Peace Exchange
P.O. Box 390
Sandy Spring, MD 20860

People to People International
501 East Armour Boulevard
Kansas City, MO 64109

The Information Department
    of the Soviet Embassy
1706 18th Street NW
Washington, DC 20009

Perhaps . . . Kids Meeting Kids
    Can Make a Difference
380 Riverside Drive
New York, NY 10025

Books

The following books will help you learn more about Mikhail Gorbachev, the Soviet Union, and important events in Soviet history. If you would like to learn more about these subjects, check your local library or bookstore to see if they have these books or if someone there can order them for you.

Lenin: Founder of the Soviet Union. Abraham Resnick
    (Childrens Press)
Mikhail Gorbachev: A Leader for Soviet Change. Walter Oleksy
    (Childrens Press)
Passport to the Soviet Union. Stephen Keeler (Franklin Watts)
The Picture Life of Mikhail Gorbachev. Janet Caulkins
    (Franklin Watts)
Portrait of the Soviet Union (series). James I. Clark (Raintree)
Portrait of the Soviet Union. Fitzroy Maclean (Henry
    Holt and Company)
The Soviet Union: The World's Largest Country. John Gillies
    (Dillon Press)

List of new words

Berlin Wall
> The barrier built by the East German government in 1961 to prevent people in East Germany from escaping to West Berlin. The Berlin Wall was torn down in November 1989.

black market
> A system of illegal trade that involves selling goods that are not available in stores.

Central Committee
> The key policy-making body within the Soviet Communist party. Within the Central Committee was a smaller group of powerful party leaders, called the Politburo.

cold war
> A period of tension and competition that exists between power groups. This term often refers to the period of this kind that existed between the Communist countries of Eastern Europe and Asia, led by the Soviet Union, and the democracies of the West, led by the United States. This cold war began after World War II and did not end until 1989.

communism
> A political system based on the belief that a nation's people as a whole — not individuals — should own the resources used to produce goods. In theory, communism's goal is to distribute wealth equally and provide for everyone's needs.

democracy
> A system of government in which power is held by the people, who elect representatives to act according to the desires of the people who voted for them.

Eastern bloc
> The nations of Eastern Europe dominated militarily, politically,

and economically by the Soviet Union from the 1940s to the late 1980s. The bloc included Poland, Czechoslovakia, Hungary, East Germany, Romania, and Bulgaria.

glasnost
The Russian word for "openness"; glasnost is one of Gorbachev's most important reforms. Under glasnost, Soviet citizens can criticize the government without fear of punishment.

Gulag
A Russian word that stands for the Chief Administration of Corrective Labor Camps; the Gulag was a system of prisons and work camps.

KGB
The Komitet Gosudarstvennoy Bezopasnosti (Committee for State Security) — an agency responsible both for controlling anti-Soviet activity within the Soviet Union and for coordinating Soviet spying and intelligence operations in other countries.

Komsomol
The Soviet Union's Communist youth movement, also called the Young Communist League.

Kremlin
The ancient walled city in the heart of Moscow that served as the seat of the Soviet government.

Lenin, Vladimir Ilyich (1870-1924)
Born Vladimir Ulyanov, Lenin was the revolutionary leader who masterminded the Communist victory in the Russian Revolution of 1917.

perestroika
The Russian word for "restructuring"; the term used for Gorbachev's plan to make the Soviet government and economy more efficient.

Politburo
   The Political Bureau of the Central Committee of the Communist party. Until Gorbachev disbanded the Communist party in 1991, the Politburo made all of the most important decisions about government policy in the Soviet Union.

republics
   The individual states — now independent nations — of the former Soviet Union.

Russia
   The largest of the former Soviet republics; now a nation.

Solidarity
   An independent labor union organized by Lech Walesa in Soviet-controlled Poland in 1980. This union helped break communism's grip on Poland, when its candidates won landslide victories in elections in 1989.

Soviet Union
   The Union of Soviet Socialist Republics, often called the USSR.

Stalin, Joseph (1879-1953)
   The Communist leader (born Iosif Vissarionovich Dzhugashvili) who in 1924 succeeded Vladimir Lenin as the political leader of the Soviet Union. He ruled the country as an absolute dictator from the late 1920s until his death in 1953.

Supreme Soviet
   Until Gorbachev's reforms, this was the Soviet Union's parliament, or law-making body.

Important dates

1905   A revolution breaks out in St. Petersburg, Russia's capital. Czar Nicholas II is forced to promise reforms. He later breaks all his promises.

1917 **March** — A revolution forces Czar Nicholas II to step down. A Western-style democracy is set up, with Aleksandr Kerensky as premier.
November — A second revolution overthrows the Kerensky government and places the Communists in control, with Vladimir I. Lenin as their leader.

1918 **July** — The czar and his family are executed.
November — World War I ends.

1924 Lenin dies.

1928 Stalin takes control of the Soviet Union. He launches a Five-Year Plan to modernize industry and agriculture.

1931 **March 2** — Mikhail Sergeyevich Gorbachev is born in Privolnoye.

1934 Stalin begins a shakeup of all levels of government, ordering death or imprisonment to anyone disloyal to him.

1941 **June 22** — German forces under dictator Adolf Hitler invade the Soviet Union.

1942 **December** — The German invaders are turned back at Stalingrad, after having conquered much of the eastern part of the Soviet Union.

1944- The Soviet armies occupy Eastern Europe, driving out the
1945 German forces. Poland, Bulgaria, Romania, Yugoslavia, Albania, and Hungary, as well as parts of Germany, come under Soviet control.

1945 World War II ends. The cold war begins.

1948 **February** — Soviet-backed Communists seize control of Czechoslovakia.

May — West Berlin is isolated by Soviet troops.
June — Yugoslavia breaks from Soviet domination and adopts a neutral position in the cold war.

1950 Gorbachev studies law at Moscow State University. While there, he meets Raisa Titorenko, whom he later marries.

1952 Gorbachev becomes a member of the Communist party.

1953 **March** — Joseph Stalin dies. He is succeeded briefly by Georgi Malenkov, who is followed by Nikita Khrushchev.

1955 After graduation from the university, Gorbachev returns to Stavropol with Raisa, where he becomes an official of the local Komsomol.

1956 The Gorbachevs' only daughter, Irina, is born.
December — Soviet troops put down a revolution against the Communist government in Hungary.

1961 **August** — The East German government builds the Berlin Wall between East and West Berlin in an effort to stop people from escaping to the non-Communist West.

1962 Gorbachev starts work as an agricultural organizer for the Communist party.

1963 Gorbachev becomes head of the agricultural department of Stavropol.

1964 Leonid Brezhnev replaces Khrushchev as general secretary.

1968 **August** — Soviet troops invade Czechoslovakia to crush a reform movement.

1969 U.S. president Richard Nixon begins a policy of friendliness and cooperation designed to ease U.S.-Soviet tensions.

1970 Gorbachev becomes the Communist party chief of the Stavropol region. He is also elected to the Supreme Soviet.

1971 Gorbachev becomes a member of the Central Committee of the Communist party.

1972 The United States and the Soviet Union sign the Strategic Arms Limitation Treaty (SALT), limiting the number of nuclear missiles on each side.

1978 Gorbachev is appointed head of the Central Committee's agricultural department.

1980 **January** — U.S. president Jimmy Carter announces an embargo on grain exports to the Soviet Union to protest the Soviet Union's invasion of Afghanistan.

1982 **November** — Brezhnev dies. KGB chief Yuri Andropov succeeds him. Gorbachev becomes Andropov's ally.

1983 **March** — Andropov suffers massive kidney failure. He survives, but is terminally ill. As Andropov's health fails, he uses Gorbachev as his representative and spokesman.

1984 **February** — Andropov dies after only fifteen months in office. Leadership passes to Konstantin Chernenko. **December 10** — Gorbachev delivers a speech in Moscow in favor of glasnost, or "openness."

1985 **March 10** — Chernenko dies. The next day, Gorbachev is named his successor. **November** — Gorbachev and U.S. president Ronald Reagan meet in Switzerland to discuss arms control and U.S.-Soviet relations.

1986 **April 26** — The world's worst nuclear accident takes place in the Ukraine at the Chernobyl nuclear power plant.

October — The second Reagan-Gorbachev summit takes place in Reykjavik, Iceland. Gorbachev suggests a ban on all nuclear weapons. Reagan rejects the proposal.

1987   His book *Perestroika* outlines Gorbachev's plans for reform.
December — At the third Reagan-Gorbachev meeting, the two leaders sign a treaty agreeing to eliminate some types of nuclear weapons.

1988   **June** — At a special party conference, Gorbachev outlines his plans to make the Soviet government more democratic.
October — Mikhail Gorbachev becomes president of the Soviet Union.

1989   Communist governments fall in Poland, Hungary, East Germany, Czechoslovakia, Bulgaria, and Romania.
December — The cold war ends.

1990   **February** — The Communist party is no longer the only party allowed in the Soviet Union.
March — Lithuania declares its independence. Gorbachev announces the move is invalid and sends troops.
June — Gorbachev meets with U.S. president George Bush, and the two agree to further arms reductions.
July — The Ukraine declares its independence. Moscow does not acknowledge this move.
October — Gorbachev sends a new economic plan to parliament. He wins the Nobel Prize for peace.

1991   **Summer/Fall** — Coup to overthrow Gorbachev fails. Gorbachev and Boris Yeltsin, president of the Russian republic, become "partners" in ruling Soviet Union. The two leaders promise swift action on reforms; Communist party no longer a force in the nation. Latvia, Lithuania, Estonia are officially recognized as independent countries.
December — Gorbachev steps down as president; union dissolves; all former republics now independent nations.

Index